PORSCHE 911 CA

MW00899942

FERRARI 360 MODENA

DODGE VIPER GTS

NISSAN SKYLINE GT-R

CHEVROLET CORVETTE STINGRAY (1960S)

FORD MUSTANG (1ª GENERACIÓN)

JAGUAR E-TYPE

ASTON MARTIN DB5

MERCEDES-BENZ
300SL GULLWING

AC COBRA

FERRARI 250 GTO

LAMBORGHINI MIURA

PORSCHE 356

ALFA ROMEO SPIDER (SERIE DUETTO)

BMW 2002

MASERATI GHIBLI (1960S)

LOTUS ESPRIT

FERRARI TESTAROSSA

AUDI QUATTRO

LANCIA DELTA INTEGRALE

TOYOTA 2000GT

FORD GT40

SHELBY MUSTANG GT500

VOLKSWAGEN BEETLE (CLÁSICO)

CITROËN DS

MINI COOPER
(ORIGINAL)

ROLLS-ROYCE SILVER SHADOW

BENTLEY CONTINENTAL R (1950S)

CADILLAC ELDORADO (1950S)

CHEVROLET CAMARO SS (1ª GENERACIÓN)

DATSUN 240Z

PONTIAC GTO

FORD THUNDERBIRD (1950S)

TRIUMPH TR6

MG MGB

FERRARI DINO 246 GT

LAMBORGHINI COUNTACH

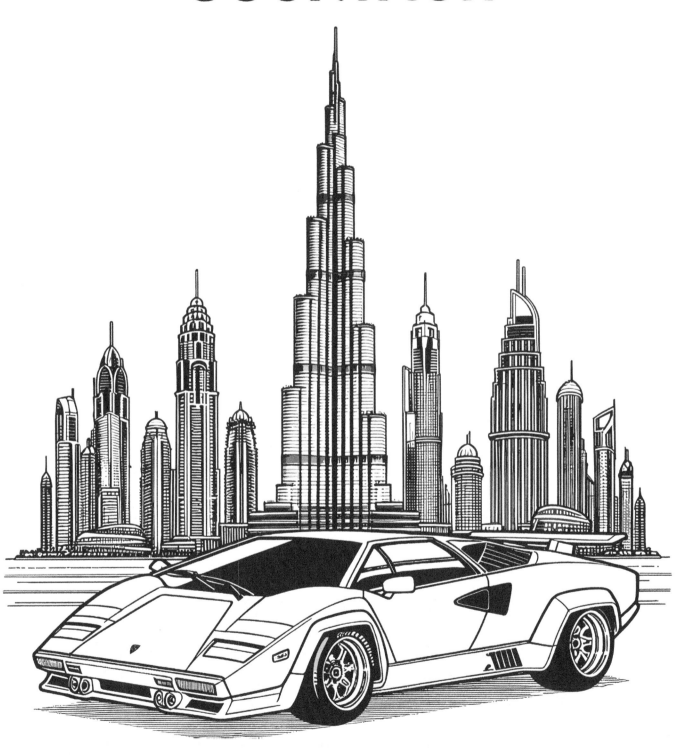

MERCEDES-BENZ 280SL

PORSCHE 914

MORGAN PLUS 8

JAGUAR XK120

ALFA ROMEO GIULIA SPRINT GT

BUICK RIVIERA
(1960S)

CADILLAC DEVILLE
(1950S)

DELOREAN DMC-12

FERRARI 308 GTS

LAMBORGHINI DIABLO

MASERATI MERAK

TOYOTA CELICA (1ª GENERACIÓN)

VOLVO P1800

1ra edición ©℗®TM 2023, Jesús Miguel Blanco Flores y Allegra Blanco Losappio impreso por Amazon

Reservados todos los derechos. Queda prohibida la reproducción total o parcial de este libro por cualquier medio o procedimiento, electrónico o mecánico, procesamiento informático, alquiler o cualquier otra forma de transmisión, sin el permiso previo por escrito de los titulares de los derechos de autor.

Asimismo, cualquier reproducción, distribución y transformación de esta obra podrá realizarse únicamente con el consentimiento de sus titulares, salvo lo dispuesto por la ley. Por favor contacte con CEDRO (Centro Español de Derechos Reprográficos) si desea fotocopiar o escanear cualquier parte de esta obra.

Made in the USA
Coppell, TX
06 April 2024

31000925R00031